Three Adventures
of Sherlock Holmes

SIR ARTH ... E

Retol... ...avid Maule
Series Editors: Andy Hopkins and Jocelyn Potter

Pearson Education Limited
Edinburgh Gate, Harlow,
Essex CM20 2JE, England
and Associated Companies throughout the world.

ISBN-13: 978-0-582-42687-0
ISBN-10: 0-582-42687-1

This edition first published 2000

7 9 10 8

Typeset by Pantek Arts Ltd, Maidstone, Kent
Set in 11/14pt Bembo
Printed in China
SWTC/07

Published by Pearson Education Limited in association with
Penguin Books Ltd, both companies being subsidiaries of Pearson Plc

Acknowledgements:
BBC Worldwide: p. 55; Granada Television: pp. 7 and 19; Scope
Features: p. 34; Transworld Features (UK) Ltd.: p. 47.

For a complete list of titles available in the Penguin Readers series, please write to your local
Pearson Education office or to: Penguin Readers Marketing Department,
Pearson Education, Edinburgh Gate, Harlow, Essex CM20 2JE.

Contents

Introduction

'Holmes,' I said, as I stood one morning at the window, looking down Baker Street, 'here is a madman coming. It seems rather sad that his relatives allow him to go out alone.'

All kinds of people visit Sherlock Holmes with their problems, and some of them are on the edge of madness when they arrive at 221b Baker Street. But Sherlock Holmes is a great detective. There are few cases that he cannot solve. Fortunately, too, his friend Dr Watson is with him, taking notes. These are Dr Watson's stories.

In 'The Speckled Band', Holmes's visitor is a very frightened young woman. Two years earlier, and only two weeks before her marriage, the young woman's twin sister died suddenly and mysteriously. Her last words were: 'It was the band! The speckled band!' Now Holmes's visitor also plans to marry, and strangely similar events are happening in her home. Will Sherlock Holmes be able to solve the puzzle in time to save her life?

In the second story, five orange pips, the seeds of the fruit, are sent to John Openshaw's uncle. Soon, the old man is dead. Then pips are sent to other members of the family. Who are they from? What do they mean? And will the deaths continue?

Holmes's visitor to Baker Street in the third story is a very successful banker. Diamonds have been stolen from him, and to his horror he believes that he knows the thief. But is he right? The banker hopes that Holmes can disprove his worst fears.

Arthur Conan Doyle's readers first met Sherlock Holmes in *A Study in Scarlet*, which appeared as a book in 1888. In the late nineteenth century, for the first time, most of the population of

England could read, and there was a great demand for entertaining fiction.

Before he became a writer, Conan Doyle studied medicine, and much of the character of Sherlock Holmes is taken from one of his teachers, Joseph Bell. When patients came to see him, Bell often told them about their jobs, their habits and perhaps their illnesses before they said a word. He taught his students the importance of small details. This is one of the skills of the great detective. Sherlock Holmes is more interested in the activities of his brain than in human emotion. He shows no interest in women, and his only friend is Dr Watson. He is often very cold.

The reading public did not seem to notice Holmes's faults. When stories about him appeared in the *Strand* magazine, he quickly became famous, and the magazine sold more copies than it had ever sold before. The three stories in this book were first printed in the *Strand*, and then appeared together in one book as *The Adventures of Sherlock Holmes* in 1892.

Conan Doyle was making money, but he wanted people to think of him as a serious writer. He wanted to write other kinds of books. So when he agreed to write a second group of stories for the *Strand*, he decided that his detective had to die. The last story ends with Holmes in Switzerland, in a terrible fight with his greatest enemy, Moriarty. When Watson arrives, both men have disappeared. They have, it seems, fallen together to their deaths.

This was not the end, of course. Conan Doyle was offered large amounts of money to write more stories about Sherlock Holmes. The result was the third full-length Holmes book, *The Hound of the Baskervilles*. However, this story takes place some time before the fight in Switzerland. Holmes's return to life came in 1903, when an American company offered the enormous sum of 25,000 dollars for six stories. Conan Doyle could not refuse, and Holmes returned to Baker Street – to the great shock of Dr Watson. It seemed that only Moriarty had died at the Falls, but Holmes had spent the next two years travelling because other men also wanted to kill him. This did not make much sense, but readers did not care. Their hero was back, and nothing else mattered. After this third group of adventures, there were two more collections of stories and a final book about Sherlock Holmes, *The Sign of Four*.

Arthur Conan Doyle was one of ten children, born into an Irish family in Edinburgh in 1859. His father, Charles Doyle, was an artist, but he drank too much and life was difficult. Young Arthur was sent away to a Catholic school in the north of England, and did not often see his father.

In 1876 he returned to Edinburgh to study medicine, but by 1890 he had stopped practising medicine and become a full-time writer. Conan Doyle died in 1930 but, like Moriarty, he had not been able to kill Sherlock Holmes. Even today, people write to the Baker Street address (now a bank), asking for the help and advice of the great detective. Sherlock Holmes never lived, but he refused to die – and, to his readers, he is still alive today.

The Speckled Band

During the past eight years I have watched my friend Sherlock Holmes at work on more than seventy cases. The most unusual is the case connected with the well-known Surrey family, the Roylotts of Stoke Moran. The events there happened not long after I first met Holmes, before my marriage, when we were sharing rooms in Baker Street.

Early in April 1883 I woke one morning and found Sherlock Holmes standing, fully dressed, by the side of my bed. He normally got up quite late, but the clock showed that it was only a quarter past seven, so I looked up at him in some surprise.

'What is it?' I asked. 'A fire?'

'No. A young lady has arrived in a great state of excitement, and wants to see me. When young ladies visit people at this early hour, I imagine that they want to talk about something very important. If this becomes an interesting case, you may want to follow it from the beginning. So I thought that I should call you.'

'My dear Holmes, I would not miss it for anything.'

My greatest pleasure was to help Holmes in his detective work, and so I quickly put on my clothes and followed him down to the sitting-room.

A lady dressed in black, wearing a thick veil, was sitting by the window. She stood up as we came into the room.

'Good morning, madam,' said Holmes cheerfully. 'My name is Sherlock Holmes. This is my friend Dr Watson. Ah, I am glad that Mrs Hudson has had the good sense to light the fire. Please come and sit beside it and I shall order you a cup of coffee. I can see that you are shaking.'

'It is not the cold that makes me shake,' said the woman quietly, changing her seat as Holmes suggested.

1

'What, then?'

'It is fear, Mr Holmes. It is terror!' She lifted her veil as she spoke. Her face was pale and her eyes were frightened, like the eyes of a hunted animal. She looked about thirty years old, but her hair was quite grey.

'You must not be afraid,' Sherlock Holmes said gently, bending forward to touch her arm. 'We shall soon be able to help, I have no doubt. You have come in by train this morning, I see.'

'You know me?'

'No, but I can see the second half of a return ticket just inside your left glove.'

'Yes, I left home before six and came in by the first train to Waterloo. Sir, I shall go mad if it continues. Only one person cares about me, and he, poor man, cannot help.

'I have heard of you, Mr Holmes, from Mrs Farintosh. You gave her help when she needed it. Oh sir, do you think that you could help me too? At the moment I cannot pay you for your services, but in a month or two I shall be married, and I shall have my own money.'

Holmes turned to his desk and, unlocking it, took out a small notebook. He studied this for a moment.

'Farintosh,' he said. 'Ah, yes, I remember the case. It was about some jewellery. I think it was before your time, Watson. I can only say, madam, that I shall be happy to give you my attention. My profession brings its own rewards. You may, though, pay my costs when you are able to. And now please tell us what your problem is.'

'Oh dear!' our visitor replied. 'The most terrible thing about my situation is that the facts seem so small and so unimportant. I have talked about this to the one man that I can call a friend. Even he thinks that it is all just in the imagination of a nervous woman. He does not say so, but I know this from the way he speaks and looks at me. But I have heard, Mr Holmes, that you can see into the human heart. You can advise me how to walk among the dangers that surround me.

'My name is Helen Stoner, and I am living with my stepfather. He is the last of one of the oldest Saxon families in England, the Roylotts of Stoke Moran, on the western border of Surrey.'

'Yes,' Holmes said, 'I have heard the name.'

'The family was once the richest in England, with very large amounts of land. In the last century, however, four oldest sons, one after another, wasted the fortunes of the family. Now there is nothing left except a small piece of land and the 200-year-old house, and a lot of money is still owed.

'The present oldest son, my stepfather, borrowed money from a relative, which allowed him to study medicine. When he became a doctor he went out to Calcutta, where he was very successful.

'However, one day some money was stolen from his house. He blamed one of his servants, and in an angry temper beat him hard until he died. He was sent to prison for many years, and afterwards returned to England, a very sad and angry man.

'When Dr Roylott was in India, he married my mother, Mrs Stoner. Her first husband, an army officer, had died. My sister Julia and I were twins, and we were only two years old at the time of my mother's remarriage. She had quite a lot of money, not less than a thousand pounds a year, and this became Dr Roylott's while we lived with him. However, she also ordered that quite a large amount of money should be ours if we got married.

'A short time after our return to England, my mother died in a railway accident near Crewe. Dr Roylott then stopped working as a doctor in London and took us to live with him in the family home at Stoke Moran. My mother's money was enough for all our needs, and there seemed no reason for us not to live happily.

'But our stepfather changed at about this time. Our neighbours were at first very happy to see a Roylott of Stoke Moran back in the old house, but he shut himself away. When he did appear, he argued with everyone.

'The men of the family have always had a violent temper. In my stepfather's case, this was made worse by his time in prison. Two terrible fights ended in the police court, and at last he became the terror of the village. He is a man of great strength, and cannot be controlled when he is angry.

'Last week he threw a local man off a bridge into a stream. This was not reported to the police only because I paid all the money that I could find. He has no friends except for some travelling people. He allows them to camp in the woods on the small piece of land we still own. They invite him into their tents, and sometimes he goes away with them for several weeks.

'He also likes Indian animals, which are sent over to him by a friend. These are feared by the villagers almost as much as their owner is.

'You can imagine that my poor sister Julia and I did not have much pleasure in our lives after our mother died. No servant stayed with us for long, and we had to do all the housework. Julia was only thirty at the time of her death, but her hair was already turning white, like mine now.'

'So your sister is dead?'

'She died two years ago, and her death is the reason that I am here. You can understand that we were very unlikely to see anyone of our own age and position. We had, however, an aunt, my mother's sister, who lives near Harrow, and we were occasionally allowed to visit her.

'Julia went there at Christmas two years ago, and she met a man who asked her to marry him. My stepfather learned of this when she returned, and seemed quite happy about the marriage.

But two weeks before the wedding day, a terrible thing happened.'

Holmes was sitting back in his chair with his eyes closed. He half opened them now, and looked across at his visitor.

'Please tell me all the details,' he said.

'It is easy for me to do that, because every event of that time is burned into my memory. The family house is, as I have already said, very old, and we now live in only one part of it. The bedrooms in this part are on the ground floor. The first room is Dr Roylott's, the second my sister's, and the third my own. There are no doors between them, but they all open into the same passage.

'The windows of these rooms open out on the garden. On the night of my sister's death, Dr Roylott had gone to his room early. However, we knew that he had not gone to bed. My sister could smell his strong Indian cigarettes.

'Because of this smell, she left her room and came into mine. She sat there for some time, talking about her wedding. At eleven o'clock she got up to leave, but she paused at the door and looked back.

'"Tell me, Helen," she said, "have you ever heard anyone whistle in the middle of the night?"

'"Never," I said.

'"You do not whistle in your sleep?"

'"Certainly not. But why?"

'"Because during the last few nights I have heard a low clear whistle, always at about three in the morning. I am a light sleeper, and it has woken me. I cannot tell where it came from — perhaps from the next room, perhaps from the garden. Have you heard it?"

'"No. It must be those travelling people in the woods."

'"Very likely. But if it was from the garden, I am surprised that you did not hear it too."

'"Ah, but I sleep more heavily than you do."

'"Well, it does not matter very much," she said, and she smiled at me and left the room. A few moments later I heard her key turn in the lock.'

'Really?' said Holmes. 'Did you always lock your doors at night?'

'Always.'

'And why?'

'I think I told you that the doctor kept some wild animals. They ran about at night. We did not feel safe unless our doors were locked.'

'I understand. Please continue.'

'I could not sleep that night. I had a feeling that something very bad was going to happen. My sister and I, you remember, were twins, and twins can be very close. It was a wild night. The wind was blowing hard outside and the rain was beating against the windows.

'Suddenly, through all the noise of the storm, I heard a wild scream. I knew that it was my sister's voice. I jumped from my bed and rushed into the passage. As I opened my door, I seemed to hear a low whistle, like the one my sister had described. A few moments later, I heard a noise like a heavy piece of metal falling.

'As I ran down the passage, my sister's door opened. By the light of the passage lamp, I saw my sister appear in the opening. Her face was white with terror.

'I ran to her and threw my arms round her, but at that moment she fell to the ground. She moved on the floor like someone in terrible pain. At first I thought she had not recognized me, but as I bent over her she suddenly screamed, "Oh, my God! Helen! It was the band! The speckled band!"

'She wanted to say something else, and she pointed in the direction of the doctor's room, but the words did not come.

'I called loudly for my stepfather, and both of us tried hard to

'I heard a wild scream. I knew that it was my sister's voice.'

save her life. We sent for medical help from the village, but there
was nothing we could do. She never opened her eyes again.'

'Was your sister dressed?' asked Holmes.

'No. She was in her nightclothes. In her right hand we found
the burnt end of a match, and in her left there was a matchbox.'

'So she struck a light and looked around her when she first
woke up. That is important. What did the police decide?'

'They were very careful, as Dr Roylott's bad behaviour had
been well known for a long time, but they were unable to find
the cause of her death. I was able to say that the door had been
locked on the inside, and the windows were closed every night.

'The walls were carefully checked, and had no hidden doors.
The police also checked the floor, with the same result. The
chimney is wide, but there are iron bars across it. It is certain,
therefore, that my sister was alone. Also, there were no marks of
violence on her.'

'What about poison?'

'The doctors examined her for it, but without success.'

'What do you think this unfortunate lady died of, then?'

'I believe that she died of fear, though I cannot imagine what frightened her so much.'

'Ah, and what did you think she meant by a band – a speckled band?'

'I do not know. Perhaps it was wild talk caused by fear. Perhaps she meant a band of people – those travellers in the woods. Many of them wear spotted handkerchiefs.'

Holmes shook his head. 'Please continue with your story,' he said.

'Two years have passed since then, and until recently my life has been a lonely one. A month ago, however, a dear friend, who I have known for many years, asked me to marry him. My stepfather has agreed to our marriage, and this will happen in the spring.

'Two days ago, some repairs were started in the west part of the building, and I have had to move into my sister's room. Imagine my terror when, last night, I suddenly heard the low whistle which she talked about on the night she died. I jumped up and lit the lamp, but I could see nothing in the room.

'I was too frightened to go to bed again, so I got dressed. When daylight came, I ran to the Crown Inn and got a carriage to Leatherhead. I have come from there this morning, to see you and to ask your advice.'

'You have been very sensible,' said my friend. 'But have you told me everything?'

'Yes, everything.'

'Miss Stoner, you have not. You are protecting your stepfather.'

'What do you mean?'

Holmes took Helen Stoner's hand, which lay on her knee, and pulled it forward a little. On her wrist were five little red spots, the marks of four fingers and a thumb.

'He has been cruel to you,' said Holmes.

The lady looked embarrassed, and covered her wrist. 'He is a difficult man,' she said, 'and perhaps he does not know his own strength.'

There was a long silence. Holmes stared into the fire.

'This is a very complicated business,' he said at last. 'There are a thousand details which I would like to know. But we cannot waste time. If we came to Stoke Moran today, would it be possible for us to see these rooms without your stepfather's knowledge?'

'Yes, I think so. He spoke of spending the whole day in London. He has some important business here.'

'Excellent. You will come with me, Watson?'

'I shall be very pleased to come.'

'I have one or two things that I would like to do since I am in London. But I shall return by the twelve o'clock train.'

'Then you will see us early in the afternoon,' Holmes said. 'Will you not eat breakfast with us?'

'No, I must go. I feel better since I have told my trouble to you. I shall look forward to seeing you again this afternoon.'

She dropped her veil over her face, and left the room.

'And what do you think of it all, Watson?' asked Sherlock Holmes, sitting back in his chair.

'It seems to me a terrible business. But the lady said that there is no way through the floor and walls. The chimney has iron bars across it, and nobody could pass through the door or the window. That means her sister was certainly alone when she met her strange death.'

'What about these whistles in the night, and the very odd words of the dying woman?'

'I have no idea.'

'I think it is possible that these travelling people had

9

something to do with it. They are close friends of the old doctor, and the doctor may want to stop his stepdaughter's marriage. Then we must think about the whistles and the speckled band. But what . . . !'

These last words were spoken because our door had suddenly been pushed open and a very large man had appeared in the room. His clothes were a strange mix. He had on the black hat and long black coat of a professional man, but his trousers were the type that you would see on a farmer. He had a thick walking stick in his hand.

His large face was very lined, burned yellow by the sun. He turned his hate-filled eyes from one to the other of us.

'Which of you is Holmes?' he asked.

'That is my name, sir,' said Holmes, 'And you are . . . ?'

'I am Dr Grimesby Roylott of Stoke Moran.'

'Really?' said Holmes quietly. 'Please take a seat.'

'No, I will not. My daughter has been here. What has she been saying to you?'

'It is a little cold for this time of year,' Holmes said.

'What has she been saying to you?' screamed the old man, now very angry.

'But the flowers are starting to appear,' continued Holmes.

'Ha! You refuse to answer?' said our new visitor, taking a step forward and waving his stick in the air. 'I know you, you troublemaker! You are Holmes, the man who cannot keep his nose out of other people's business.' My friend smiled. 'Holmes, the man who pretends to be a policeman!'

Holmes laughed loudly. 'Your conversation is very entertaining,' he said. 'When you leave, please close the door.'

'I will leave when I have said what I want to say. Stay away from my business. I know that Miss Stoner has been here – I had her followed! I am a dangerous man! Look.' He stepped quickly forward, picked up the poker, and bent it into a curve with his large brown hands. Then, throwing the poker into the fireplace, he marched out of the room.

'He seems to be a very nice man,' Holmes said, laughing. 'I am not quite so big, but I think my strength is almost as great as his.' As he spoke, he picked up the poker. With a sudden pull on each end, he straightened it again.

'This makes the whole case more interesting,' he added. 'I only hope that our little friend will not suffer because she came here. And now, Watson, we shall order breakfast, and afterwards I shall go to the records office. I hope to get some useful information there.'

It was nearly one o'clock when Sherlock Holmes returned. He held in his hand a sheet of blue paper, with notes and figures written on it.

'I have seen the will of the dead wife,' he said. 'There is a large sum of money which, eight years ago, produced about £1,100 a year. Now, because of the fall in farming prices, the amount is probably less than £750. And when a daughter marries, she will receive £250 a year.

'So, if both girls – or even one girl – married, there would be little money for him. My morning's work has not been wasted. He has very strong reasons for stopping their marriages.

'Watson, this is very serious, and the old man knows that we are interested in his business. If you are ready, we will call a carriage and drive to Waterloo. Please bring your revolver. It may be necessary to use it.'

At Waterloo we caught a train for Leatherhead, where we hired a carriage at the station inn. We drove through the lovely Surrey country roads. It was a perfect day, with a bright sun and a few light clouds in the sky. The trees were just beginning to show their new leaves, and the air was full of the pleasant smell of the wet earth. There was a big difference between the beauty of the spring and the dark business which had brought us here.

My friend sat in the front of the carriage, thinking hard. His hat was pulled down over his eyes, and his chin was on his chest. Suddenly, however, he sat up, touched me on the shoulder, and pointed over the fields at a large, very old grey house.

'Look there,' he said. 'Stoke Moran.'

'Yes sir, that is the house of Dr Grimesby Roylott,' said the driver.

'There is some building work there,' said Holmes. 'That is where we are going.'

'There's the village,' said the driver, pointing to a group of roofs a little way away, 'but the footpath through the fields is quicker. There it is, where the lady is walking.'

'And the lady, I think, is Miss Stoner,' said Holmes.

We got off, and paid our fare, and the carriage turned back on its way to Leatherhead.

'I thought,' said Holmes, 'that the driver should think we had come here as builders, or on some definite business. It may stop him talking. Good afternoon, Miss Stoner.'

Our visitor of the morning hurried forward to meet us. 'I've been waiting for you,' she cried, shaking hands with us warmly. 'Everything is going well. Dr Roylott has gone to London and is unlikely to be back before evening.'

'We have already met the doctor,' said Holmes, and in a few words he told her what had happened.

Miss Stoner turned white as she listened.

'Oh no!' she cried. 'He has followed me, then?'

'You must lock yourself away from him tonight. If he is violent, we shall take you away to your aunt's at Harrow. Now, we must make the best use of our time. Please take us to the rooms which we need to examine.'

The house was built of grey stone, with a central part and two curving side parts. The windows on one side were broken, and covered with wooden boards. The central part was in better condition, but the part on the right-hand side was quite modern. This was where the family lived.

Some building work was being done on the end wall, but there were no workmen at the time of our visit. Holmes carefully examined the outsides of the windows.

'This, I believe, belongs to your old room, the centre one to your sister's, and the one next to the main building belongs to Dr Roylott's bedroom?'

'Yes, but I am now sleeping in the middle room.'

'Because of the building work, as I understand. I can see no great need for repairs to that end wall.'

'The work is unnecessary. I believe that it is an excuse to move me from my room.'

'Ah! That is interesting. Now, would you please go into your room, and lock the shutters.'

Miss Stoner did so. Holmes took out a knife and tried to force the shutter open, but without success.

'Hmm,' he said. 'No one could get through these shutters if the iron bars were in place, locking them. Well, perhaps the inside of the room will give us some ideas.'

A small side-door led into the white painted passage. We went first into the middle room, where Miss Stoner was now sleeping.

It was quite small, with a low ceiling and a wide fireplace. A brown chest of drawers stood in one corner, a narrow bed in another, and a table on the left-hand side of the window. The only other furniture was two small chairs.

The walls were covered with wood, which looked about the same age as the house. Holmes pulled one of the chairs into a corner and sat silently. His eyes moved around, examining every detail of the room.

'When that bell rings, who answers it?' he asked at last. He pointed to a thick bell rope which hung down beside the bed. The end of it was actually lying on the pillow.

'It goes to the servant's room.'

'It looks newer than everything else in the room.'

'Yes, it was only put there two years ago.'

'Your sister asked for it, I suppose?'

'No, she never used it. When we wanted something, we got it ourselves.'

'Then it does not seem necessary to have such a nice bell rope there. Please excuse me for a few minutes while I look at this floor.'

He lay face-down and examined the spaces between the boards. Then he did the same with the wood around the walls. He walked to the bed and stared at it. Finally, he took the bell rope in his hand and pulled it.

'It is not a real bell!' he said. 'This is very interesting. It is fixed to the wall just above the ventilator.'

'How silly! I have never noticed that before.'

'Very strange!' said Holmes quietly, pulling at the rope. 'There are one or two unusual things about this room. For example, why does that ventilator go into another room, when it could open to the outside air?'

'That is also quite modern,' the lady said.

'Was it put in at about the same time as the bell rope?' Holmes asked.

'Yes, there were several little changes at that time.'

'Bell ropes which do not pull, and ventilators which do not ventilate. Now, with your permission, Miss Stoner, we will move next door.'

Dr Roylott's room was larger than Helen's, but it also had little furniture in it. There was a bed, a small wooden shelf of books, an armchair beside the bed, a plain wooden chair against the wall, a round table, and a large iron box. Holmes walked slowly round and round, examining everything with great interest.

'What is in here?' he asked, touching the box.

'My stepfather's business papers.'

'Oh! You have seen inside?'

'Only once. Some years ago. I remember it was full of papers.'

'There is not a cat in it, for example?'

'No. What a strange idea!'

'Well, look at this!' He picked up a small bowl of milk which was on top of it.

'No, we do not keep a cat, but there are some larger animals around.'

'Ah yes, of course. But this is a very small bowl. Now, I would like to check one thing.'

He bent down in front of the wooden chair, and examined it closely.

'Thank you. That is fine,' he said, standing up straight again. 'Ah! Here is something interesting.'

He had seen a small dog lead, hanging on one corner of the bed. The end of it was tied in a small circle.

'What do you think of that, Watson?'

'It is an ordinary lead. But I do not know why it is tied.'

'That is not so normal, is it? Well, I think I have seen enough now, Miss Stoner. With your permission, we shall walk in the garden again.'

When we left the room, my friend's face was more serious than I have ever seen it. We walked several times up and down the garden before he spoke.

'Miss Stoner, you must follow my advice completely. If you do not, you may die.'

'I shall do what you want me to do.'

'First, my friend and I must spend the night in your room.'

Both Miss Stoner and I looked at him in surprise.

'Yes, we must. Let me explain. I believe that is the village inn over there?'

'Yes, that is the Crown.'

'Very good. Your windows can be seen from there?'

'Certainly.'

'You must stay in your room when your stepfather comes back. When he goes to his room for the night, you must open the shutters of your window and put your lamp there so we can see it. Then you must go into your old bedroom. I am sure that you can manage there for one night.'

'Oh, yes, easily.'

'We will spend the night in your room. We will try to discover the reason for the noise that you have heard.'

'I believe, Mr Holmes, that you already know the answer,' said Miss Stoner, placing her hand on my friend's arm.

'Perhaps I do.'

'Then please tell me the cause of my sister's death.'

'I would prefer to be more certain before I speak.'

'Do you think she died of fear?'

'No, I do not think so. I think there was probably a more real cause. And now, Miss Stoner, we must leave you. If Dr Roylott returned and saw us, our journey would be for nothing. Goodbye, and be brave.'

Sherlock Holmes and I took a bedroom and a sitting-room at the Crown Inn. They were upstairs on the first floor, and from our window we could see the house quite easily. Early in the evening we saw Dr Roylott drive past in a carriage. A few minutes later, there was a sudden light among the trees as the lamp was lit in one of the sitting-rooms.

'Watson,' said Holmes, as we sat together in the growing darkness, 'I am unsure about taking you tonight. I think there may be some danger.'

'Can I help?'

'You might be very useful.'

'Then I shall certainly come. I think you saw more in those rooms than I could see.'

'Well, I knew that we would find a ventilator before we even came to the house.'

'My dear Holmes!'

'Oh, yes, I did. Helen Stoner said that her sister could smell the smoke of Dr Roylott's cigarettes. That, of course, suggested that there must be an opening between the two rooms. It could only be a small one, because the police did not report it. It had to be a ventilator.'

'But is that important?'

'Don't you think it is strange?' Holmes asked me. 'A ventilator is put in, a bell rope is hung, and the lady in the bed dies. Did you notice that the bed was fixed to the floor? The lady could not move her bed. It had to stay there – near the bell rope, and under the ventilator.'

'Holmes,' I cried, 'I am beginning to understand! We must stop a clever and horrible crime.'

'Yes, when a doctor becomes a criminal, he is the worst of criminals. He has all the knowledge that is necessary for murder. I think we may have a terrible night ahead of us. For the moment, let us have a quiet pipe and try to think about something more cheerful.'

At about nine o'clock, the light among the trees went out, and the house went dark. Two hours passed slowly, and then, suddenly, a single bright light shone out.

'That is our sign,' said Holmes, jumping to his feet. 'It comes from the middle window.'

A moment later, we were out on the dark road. When we got near the house, we left the road and walked through the trees. We reached the garden, walked quietly through it and climbed into the bedroom. Holmes silently closed the shutters. Then he moved the lamp on to the table and looked around the room. It seemed just the same as before.

He came close to me and, speaking in a whisper, said, 'The

smallest sound could ruin all our plans. We must sit without a light. He would see it through the ventilator. Do not go to sleep. Your life may be in danger. Have your revolver ready. I will sit on the side of the bed, and you in that chair.'

I took out my revolver and put it on the corner of the table. Holmes had brought a long thin stick, and he placed this on the bed beside him. Near it he put a box of matches and the end of a candle. Then he turned down the lamp and we were left in the dark.

How shall I ever forget the terrible hours that followed? Sometimes, from outside, we heard the cry of a night bird, and the church clock struck every quarter of an hour. Twelve o'clock passed, and one, and two, and three. We still sat silently, waiting for something to happen.

Suddenly, a light shone for a moment in the direction of the ventilator. It disappeared immediately, but it was followed by a strong smell of burning oil and heated metal. Someone in the next room had lit a small lamp. I heard a gentle sound of movement, and then everything was silent again, though the smell grew stronger.

For half an hour I sat listening. Then I heard something else – a very gentle sound like steam escaping from a pot. Holmes jumped from the bed and lit the candle. Then he struck wildly with his stick at the bell rope.

'Can you see it, Watson?' he shouted. 'Can you see it?'

But I saw nothing. When Holmes struck the match, I heard a low clear whistle. But the sudden light made it impossible to see what my friend was striking. I could, however, see that his face was pale and filled with horror.

Holmes had now put down his stick, and he was looking up at the ventilator. Then came the most horrible cry I have ever heard. It was a scream of pain and anger, and it grew louder and louder. They say that, down in the village, sleepers jumped from

Then he struck wildly with his stick at the bell rope.

their beds. I stood staring at Holmes, and he at me, until it stopped.

'What does that mean?' I said.

'It means that it is finished,' Holmes answered. 'And perhaps it is the best thing that could happen. Take your revolver, and we will enter Dr Roylott's room.'

Holmes lit the lamp, and led the way down the passage. Twice he knocked on the door of the room, but there was no reply. Then he turned the handle and entered. I was just behind him, with the revolver in my hand.

On the table stood a small lamp. The iron box was open and near it, on the wooden chair, sat Dr Grimesby Roylott. On his knees lay the dog lead which we had noticed earlier. Dr Roylott's eyes were fixed in a terrible stare. Round his head there was a strange yellow band with brown spots.

'The band! The speckled band!' whispered Holmes.

I took a step forward. The band moved, and I saw it was a snake.

'That is the most dangerous type of snake in India!' Holmes cried. 'He died seconds after it bit him.'

As he spoke, he took the dog lead quickly from the dead man's knees, put the circle round the snake's head, and threw it into the iron box.

These are the true facts of the death of Dr Grimesby Roylott of Stoke Moran. We told the news to the sad girl, then took her by the morning train to her aunt in Harrow. We then called the police. They decided that the doctor had died while playing with a dangerous pet.

On the train the next day, Sherlock Holmes told me the facts that I still had to learn about the case.

'At first,' he said, 'I had completely the wrong idea. I thought the dead girl meant a "band" of travelling people. However, when I saw that nobody could get into that room through the window or the door, I had to think again.

'There were three strange things in the room – the ventilator the bell rope and the bed. I decided that the rope might be a bridge for something that passed through the ventilator to the bed.

'The idea of a snake came to me because I knew that the doctor had a number of animals from India. He is also a doctor, and has worked in India, so he would know about poison that is not discovered by any test. Another advantage of a snake is the speed with which the poison works. No policeman would notice the two little holes where it went in.

'Then I thought of the whistle. Of course, he had to get the snake back before daylight. He had taught it, possibly using the bowl of milk, to return to him when he whistled. So every night, very late, he put it through the ventilator. It climbed down the rope and landed on the bed. It might or might not bite the sleeping girl. Perhaps she might escape every night for a week, but sooner or later it would kill her.

'I decided all this before I even entered his room. I examined his chair and saw that he had often stood on it. He used it, of course, to reach the ventilator. When I saw the iron box, the bowl of milk and the dog lead, I was sure that I had the right idea. Miss Stoner had spoken about the sound of falling metal. That was when the doctor quickly shut the iron box after he had put the snake inside.

'So then we had to see if I was right. When I heard a hissing sound, I knew that the snake was coming through. I quickly lit the candle and attacked it.'

'And it went back through the ventilator.'

'Yes, and then it bit Dr Roylott. I am responsible for his death, but I do not feel very guilty about that.'

The Five Orange Pips

When I look back over my records of Sherlock Holmes's cases between the years 1882 and 1890, I find many that were strange and interesting. It is difficult to know which cases to include here. Some have already been reported in the newspapers, and others did not allow my friend to show his very special abilities. There are others which he could not solve or which never completely satisfied him. One of these cases was very unusual in its details. I will tell what I know of the story.

It began on an evening in September 1887, during a very violent autumn storm. All day the wind had screamed and the rain had beaten against the windows. As evening came, the storm grew louder and louder, and the wind cried like a child in the chimney.

Sherlock Holmes walked up and down, checking records of his past cases. I sat at the desk, organising some medical notes. My wife was visiting her aunt, and for a few days I was living in my old rooms in Baker Street.

'Was that the door bell?' I said, looking up at my friend. 'Who would come tonight?'

'If someone needs my help, it must be a serious case,' Holmes agreed.

At that moment, there was a knock at the door. Holmes turned a lamp towards the chair on which the visitor would sit.

'Come in!' he said.

The man was young, perhaps twenty-two years old or less, and well dressed. His wet umbrella and his long shining raincoat showed the wild weather that he had come through. He looked around anxiously in the bright light of the lamp, and I could see that his face was pale and his eyes were heavy. He was a very worried man.

'I must ask you to forgive me for visiting you so late,' he said, putting on a pair of gold glasses. 'I am sorry, too, that I have brought some of the bad weather into this warm room.'

'You have come from Sussex, I see,' Holmes said.

'Yes, from Horsham.'

'That mud on your shoes is quite typical of the area.'

'I have come for advice.'

'That is easy.'

'And help.'

'That is not always so easy.'

'I have heard of you, Mr Holmes. I heard from Captain Prendergast how you saved him in that business at the Tankerville Club.'

'Ah, of course. They said that he cheated at cards. They were wrong.'

'He said that you could solve anything – that you are never beaten.'

'I have been beaten – three times by men and once by a woman. But it is true that I have generally been successful. Please pull your chair closer to the fire, and tell me some details of your case.'

'It is not an ordinary one.'

'I expected that. People come to me after they have tried everything else. They do not bring me ordinary cases. Now, please give us the facts from the beginning.'

The young man moved his chair and pushed his wet feet out towards the fire.

'My name,' he said, 'is John Openshaw, but this awful business is a family matter. To give you an idea of the facts, I must go back to the beginning.

'My grandfather had two sons – my uncle Elias and my father Joseph. My father had a small factory in Coventry. He made parts for bicycles, and was successful. After some years he sold the business for quite a lot of money.

'My uncle Elias went to America when he was a young man, and became a planter in Florida. At the time of the war between the northern and southern states, he fought in Jackson's army. When the South was beaten, he returned to Florida and stayed there for three or four years. In about 1869 or 1870, he came back to Europe and bought some land in Sussex, near Horsham. He had made a lot of money in the United States, but he left because black people had been allowed to vote. He did not like that.

'He was an unusual man, often angry and bad-tempered, and he did not seem to like other people. He lived near Horsham for years, but I do not think that he ever went into the town. He had a garden and two or three fields around the house. He took his exercise there, though very often he did not leave his room for several weeks. He drank a lot and smoked very heavily, and he did not want any friends, not even his own brother.

'But he seemed to like me. I first saw him when I was only about twelve. I think that was in the year 1878 – he had been in England for eight or nine years. He asked my father to let me come and live with him, and he was very kind to me in his way. I spoke to other people for him, and at sixteen I was almost completely in charge of the house. I kept all the keys and looked after the money. I could go where I liked and do what I liked.

'There was only one place where I was not allowed to go. That was a locked room at the top of the house. Because I was like any other boy, I looked through the keyhole, but I was only able to see a collection of old boxes.

'One day – in March 1883 – a letter with a foreign stamp lay on the table in front of Uncle Elias's plate. He did not often receive letters, because his bills were paid in cash and he had no friends.

'"From India!" he said, as he picked it up. "Pondicherry postmark! What can this be?" He opened the letter and out fell five little seeds – orange pips. I began to laugh at this, but my laugh died at the sight of his face. His lip had fallen, his eyes stared and his skin turned pale. He held the letter in a shaking hand. "K.K.K!" he cried, and then: "My God, my God! My past has found me."

'"What is it, uncle?" I cried.

'"Death!" he said. Then he got up from the table and left the room, leaving me puzzled and very afraid. I picked up the envelope. Inside, in red ink, the letter "K" was written three times. There was nothing else except the five dried pips. What could the reason be for his great terror? I left the breakfast table and met him coming downstairs. He had a large key in one hand and a small box, like a cash box, in the other.

'"They can do what they like, but I will win in the end," he said angrily. "Tell Mary" – she was his servant – "that I shall want a fire in my room today, and send for Fordham, my lawyer."

'I did as he ordered. When the lawyer arrived, I asked him to come up to the room. The fire was burning brightly and all around it there were black pieces of burnt paper. The small box stood open and empty beside it. As I looked at the box I noticed, with surprise, that there were three Ks printed on it.

'"I want you, John," my uncle said, "to witness my will. I am leaving my house and my land, with all its advantages and disadvantages, to my brother, your father. When he dies it will, no doubt, come to you. If you can enjoy my money in peace, that is good! If you cannot, leave everything to your worst enemy. I do not know what is going to happen. Please sign the paper where Mr Fordham shows you."

'I signed the will and the lawyer took it away with him. This strange event puzzled me. I could not escape from a feeling of fear, though this grew less strong as the weeks passed and nothing happened to affect our lives.

'But I could see a change in my uncle. He drank more than before, and he spent most of the time in his room, with the door locked on the inside. Sometimes he got drunk and ran around the garden with a gun in his hand, shouting that he was afraid of nobody. Then he rushed back into the house, locking the door behind him.

'Well, one night he ran out of the house like this, but he never came back. When we went to search for him, we found him face downwards in a small lake at the bottom of the garden. There was no sign of a fight, and the water was only two feet deep.

'He was dead, and the police believed that he had killed himself. He had behaved strangely for months. But I did not believe this. I knew how much he was afraid of death. Time passed, however, and my father now owned the house, the land, and fourteen thousand pounds in the bank.'

'One moment,' Holmes said. 'Your story is one of the strangest I have ever heard. When did your uncle receive the letter, and when did he die?'

'The letter arrived on 10th March, 1883. His death was seven weeks later, on the night of May 2nd.'

'Thank you. Please continue.'

'When my father first came to the house, I asked him to examine the room which had always been kept locked. We found the small box there, but it was empty except for one piece of paper. It had the letters K.K.K. on it, and the words "Letters, receipts and list of members".

'These were probably the papers that my uncle destroyed. There was nothing else important in the room – only papers and notebooks connected with my uncle's life in America. Some of these showed that he had been a good soldier during the war.

Others, from after this time, were about politics. They showed that he had been strongly against the politicians who had been sent down from the North.

'Well, my father came to live at Horsham in 1884, and all went well until January of 1885. On the fourth day after New Year, I heard a shout of surprise from my father. He was sitting at the breakfast table with an open envelope in one hand and five dried orange pips in the other. He had always laughed at my story about Uncle Elias, but now he looked very puzzled and frightened.

'"What does this mean, John?" he whispered.

'"It is the K.K.K," I said. I was frightened too.

'He looked inside the envelope. "Yes, here are the same letters. But what is written above them?"

'"Put the papers on the stone seat," I read, looking over his shoulder.

'"What papers? What stone seat?" he asked.

'"The stone seat in the garden? But the papers have been destroyed."

'"This is rubbish," he said, beginning to sound braver. "This sort of thing does not happen in this country. Where does this letter come from?"

'"From Dundee," I answered, looking at the postmark.

'"A stupid joke," he said. "Why should they write to me about stone seats and papers?"

'"I think you should speak to the police," I said.

'"They will laugh at me. No, I can't do that."

'"Then let me speak to them."

'"No, let's not do anything."

'I could not change his mind, but I was very worried about the letter.

'Three days later, my father decided to visit a friend who lived a few miles away. I was happy about this, because I thought that he was in less danger when he was away from home. But I was wrong. On the second day, I received a message. My father had fallen into a deep hole in the ground. He was still breathing when I got to him, but he could not speak. He died soon after that.

'He did not know the country, and there was no fence around the hole, so the police decided that his death was an accident.

'I, too, could find nothing that suggested murder. There were no signs of a fight, no footprints. Nothing had been stolen from his pockets and no strangers had been seen in the area. But, of course, I still believed that someone had killed him.

'In this strange way I became the owner of the house and the land. I did not sell it and move away because I believe that the problems are connected with something in my uncle's life. The danger would, I think, be as great in another house.

'My poor father was killed in January 1885, and two years and eight months have passed since then. I have lived happily at Horsham, but yesterday morning it all started again.'

The young man took an envelope from his pocket. Turning to the table, he shook out five dried orange pips.

'This is the envelope,' he continued. 'The postmark is London – the East End. Inside are the same words that were in my father's envelope – "K.K.K.", and then, "Put the papers on the stone seat." '

'What have you done?' asked Holmes.

'Nothing.'

'Nothing?'

'I feel completely helpless.' He let his face fall into his thin, white hands. 'I seem to be in great danger, and nothing can save me from it. But I have seen the police.'

'Ah?'

'They listened to my story with a smile. I think they believe that the letters were jokes, and the deaths of my uncle and father were just accidents. However, they have given me a policeman, who can stay in the house with me.'

'Has he come with you tonight?'

'No. He was ordered to stay in the house.'

'Stupid!' Holmes said. 'So why did you come to me? And why did you not come immediately?'

'I only spoke to Captain Prendergast about my problem today, and he told me to come and see you.'

'It is two days since you received the letter, and too much time has passed already. Have you anything else that could help us?'

'There is one thing,' said John Openshaw. He put his hand in his pocket and took out a piece of light blue paper. 'After my uncle burned his papers, I found this on the floor of his room. Perhaps he dropped it when he took the others to the fire. I think it is a page from a private diary. The writing is certainly my uncle's.'

Holmes moved the lamp, and we both bent over the sheet of paper. The irregular edge showed that it had been torn from a book. It had 'March 1869' at the top, and underneath this was written:

4th	Hudson came.
5th	Sent the pips to McCauley, Paramore and John Swain of St Augustine.
9th	Paramore left.
10th	John Swain left.
12th	Visited Paramore. All well.

'Thank you,' said Holmes, giving the paper back to our visitor. 'And now you must not lose another moment. You must go home immediately, and act.'

'What shall I do?'

'You must put this piece of paper into the box which you have described. You must also put in a note to say that all the other papers were burned by your uncle. After that, you must put the box out on the stone seat, as they said. Do you understand?'

'Completely.'

'First, we must take away the danger that you are in. Second, we must solve the mystery, and punish the guilty ones.'

'Thank you,' said the young man, standing up and putting on his coat. 'You have given me new hope. I shall certainly do as you advise.'

'Don't waste any time. And take care of yourself. How will you go home?'

'By train from Waterloo Station.'

'It is not yet nine. The streets are still crowded, so I think that you may be safe. Remember to guard yourself well.'

'I am carrying a gun.'

'That is good. Tomorrow I shall start work on your case.'

'I shall see you at Horsham, then?'

'No. Your secret lies in London. I shall look for it here.'

'Then I shall come in a day, or in two days, with news of the box and the papers.'

He shook hands with us and left. Outside, the wind still screamed, and the rain was beating against the windows.

Sherlock Holmes sat in silence, with his head down and his eyes on the fire. Then he lit his pipe and looked up.

'I think, Watson,' he said, 'that this is the most puzzling of our cases.'

'Well, yes,' I said.

'This John Openshaw seems to be in great danger.'

'But have you,' I asked, 'any definite ideas about those dangers? Who is this K.K.K., and why is he destroying this unhappy family?'

'I have always said that a man should only keep in his brain what he needs to know from day to day. When something unusual comes along, like the meaning of K.K.K., he can always go to his library.'

He got out of his chair and crossed to the shelf where he kept his books on America. He found the one he wanted. He sat down again, placed it on his knee, but didn't open it.

'Now,' he said, 'first, we can guess that Elias Openshaw had a very strong reason for leaving America. Men of his age do not change their way of life, or willingly leave the warm weather of Florida for the lonely life of an English town. He wanted to be alone in England, which suggests that he was frightened of someone or something. So then we need to think about the three letters. Do you remember the postmarks?'

'The first was from Pondicherry, the second from Dundee, and the third from London.'

'From East London. What does that tell you?'

'They are all sea ports. Probably the writer was on a ship.'

'Excellent. And in the case of Pondicherry, Elias was killed seven weeks after receiving the letter. The Dundee letter arrived only three or four days before a death. Dundee, of course, is nearer. I think the men came on a sailing ship, and they always sent their warning ahead of them. It probably arrived before them because it came on a steamship, as letters usually do.'

'It is possible.'

'More than that,' said Holmes. 'It is probably what happened. And now you see the danger that John Openshaw is in. This letter comes from London and therefore we cannot expect any delay.'

'Good God!' I cried. 'What can it mean, this endless killing?'

'Elias Openshaw's papers are of great importance to the persons in the sailing ship. I say "persons" because it would be difficult for a single man to kill two men and make both deaths look like accidents.

'These men want their papers back, and they will kill whoever has them. So K.K.K. is not the name of a person, but of a society.'

'But of what society?'

'Have you never– ' said Sherlock Holmes, bending forward and talking in a low voice – 'have you never heard of the Ku Klux Klan?'

'No, I have not.'

Holmes turned the pages of the book on his knee. 'Here it is,' he said after a moment. '"Ku Klux Klan. This terrible secret society was started by some soldiers in the southern states after the end of the war, and it quickly spread to different parts of the country, especially Tennessee, Louisiana, the Carolinas, Georgia and Florida.

"Its power was used for political purposes, mainly to frighten black voters. It murdered people who were against its views. When a murder was planned, a warning was usually sent – leaves from a certain tree in some parts, apple seeds or orange pips in others. The man could then change his ways, or leave the country. If he took no notice of the warning, he was killed.

"The society was very well-organized, so few of its members were ever brought to court. For some years the Ku Klux Klan was very strong. The United States Government, and the better type of people in the South, could do nothing about it. Then, in the year 1869, it stopped operating, though there have been some examples of the same sort of crime since that date."

'You see,' said Holmes, putting down the book, 'the sudden end of the society's power came at the same time as Openshaw disappeared from America with their papers. It is not surprising that he and his family have been hunted ever since then. The list of names may include some of the most important men in the South. There may be many men who will not sleep easily at night until they get it back.'

'Then the page which we have seen–'

'It said, if I remember correctly, "sent the pips to A, B and C" – so the society's warning was sent to them. Then it says that A and B "left" the country, and finally C was visited, and probably killed.

'Young Openshaw must do what I have told him. It is his only chance. But we can do nothing more tonight, so I shall play my violin. Let us try to forget for half an hour this terrible weather, and the even more terrible ways of men.'

The next morning, the sun was shining a little through the veil of fog which always hangs over the great city. Sherlock Holmes was already at breakfast when I came down.

'Please excuse me,' he said. 'I did not wait, because I have, I think, a very busy day in front of me.'

'What will you do?' I asked.

'I may have to go down to Horsham.'

'But you will not go there first?'

'No, I shall begin here in London. Just ring the bell for some coffee.'

As I waited, I lifted the unopened newspaper from the table and looked at the front page.

'Holmes!' I cried. 'You are too late!'

'Ah,' he said, putting down his cup. 'I was afraid so. How was it done?' He spoke calmly, but I could see that he felt deeply about it.

'Here is the story: "Between nine and ten last night, a policeman heard a cry for help near Waterloo Bridge. He then heard the sound of something falling into the water. A number of people tried to help, but the night was very dark and stormy. It was impossible to do anything.

'"After some time the river police managed to pull the body out of the water. An envelope was found in his pocket. This told the police that the young man's name was John Openshaw, and that his house was near Horsham. There were no signs of

'Young Openshaw must do what I have told him. It is his only chance.'

violence on his body. It is possible that, on his way to Waterloo station, he walked into the river by mistake in the dark.

'"We suggest building some fences along the sides of the river near Waterloo Bridge."'

We sat in silence for some minutes. Holmes was more affected than I had ever seen him.

'This really hurts me, Watson,' he said at last. 'It has become a personal matter now, and I shall put my hand on the men who did this. That young man came to me for help, and I sent him away to his death!'

He jumped from his chair, and walked up and down the room. His face, normally pale, was very red.

'They must be very clever,' he said. 'How did they make him go down there? The riverside is not on the way to the station. Well, Watson, we shall see who will win in the end. I am going out now!'

'To the police?'

'No. After I catch them, the police can have them.'

All day I was busy with medical matters, and I did not return to Baker Street until late in the evening. Sherlock Holmes had not come back yet. It was nearly ten o'clock before he entered, looking pale and tired. He walked to the side table, pulled a piece from the loaf of bread, and ate it hungrily.

'You are hungry,' I said.

'Very. I have had nothing to eat since breakfast. I had no time.'

'And have you been successful?'

'Very.'

'You know who the men are?'

'Yes, young Openshaw's death will be paid for. And I think we shall send them a warning that they will recognize.'

'What do you mean?'

He took an orange from the cupboard, and squeezed out the pips onto the table. He took five of them and pushed them into an envelope. On the inside he wrote, 'S.H. for J.O.' Then he closed it and addressed it to 'Captain James Calhoun, Sailing Ship *Lone Star*, Savannah, Georgia, USA.'

'That will be there before him. He can read it when he arrives,' he said, laughing. 'It may give him a sleepless night.'

'And who is this Captain Calhoun?'

'The leader of these men. I shall get the others too, but he is the first.'

'How did you find him?'

'I have spent the whole day,' Holmes said, 'at the port of London. I have studied the lists of all the ships which were at Pondicherry in January and February 1883. There were thirty-six large ships. Of these, the *Lone Star* caught my attention, because it was an American ship.'

'What then?'

'I studied the records for Dundee, and I found that the *Lone Star* was there in January 1885. I knew that I had the right ship. I then checked the ships which are at the moment in the port of London.'

'Yes?'

'The *Lone Star* arrived here last week. I went to have a look at her, but she sailed early this morning.'

'What will you do, then?'

'Oh, I have my hand on him. Captain Calhoun and the two other officers are the only three Americans on the ship. The others are Finns and Germans. I also know that all three of them were away from the ship last night. I learnt that from one of the workers in the port. I expect the mail boat to carry this letter to Savannah before their sailing ship arrives. I will also send a message to the Savannah police that these three gentlemen are wanted here for murder.'

The murderers of John Openshaw, however, never received

the orange pips. They did not know that another, much cleverer person, was hunting for them.

The autumn storms that year were very bad. For a long time we waited for news of the *Lone Star* of Savannah, but none reached us. We did at last hear that a broken piece of wood from a boat was found on the water, far out in the Atlantic. The letters L.S. were cut into it, and that is all we know about the end of the *Lone Star*.

The Crown of Diamonds

Part 1   The Banker's Problem

'Holmes,' I said, as I stood one morning at the window, looking down Baker Street, 'here is a madman coming. It seems rather sad that his relatives allow him to go out alone.'

My friend got up from his armchair and looked over my shoulder. It was a bright cold February morning, and snow lay deep on the ground, shining in the winter sun.

The man was about fifty years old, tall, rather fat, and well dressed in expensive clothes. But his behaviour did not suit his clothes; as he ran along the street, he waved his arms up and down and shook his head.

'What is the matter with him?' I asked. 'Is he looking up at the numbers of the houses?'

'I believe he is coming here, my dear Watson,' said Holmes.

'Here?'

'Yes, I think he may want to speak to me professionally. Ha!' As he spoke, the man rushed at our door and pulled our bell, making a great noise.

A few moments later, he was in our room. He was breathing hard and waving his arms in the air. But we stopped smiling when we saw the sadness in his eyes.

For a time, he could not speak. His body moved from side to side and he pulled at his hair like a madman. Sherlock Holmes pushed him gently down into a chair.

'You have come to tell me your story, haven't you?' he said. 'Please wait until you feel better, and then tell me about your problem.'

The man sat silently until his breathing slowed down. Then he turned towards us.

'You probably think I am mad,' he said. 'I have a problem that is enough to make me mad. I could live with public shame, although my character has never been questioned. Private problems are also common. But the two have come together, in a terrible way, and have almost destroyed me. Also, I am not alone. The most important people in the country will suffer too, unless you can find a way out of this horrible business.'

'Calm yourself, sir,' said Holmes. 'Who are you, and what has happened to you?'

'My name,' answered our visitor, 'is probably familiar to you. I am Alexander Holder, of the banking company Holder & Stevenson, of Threadneedle Street.'

The name was well known to us. This man was the older partner of the second largest private bank in the City of London. What had happened, then, to bring one of London's leading citizens to this sad situation? We waited until he managed to begin his story.

'Time is valuable, so I hurried when the police suggested I should ask for your help. I take very little exercise, but carriages are too slow in this snow, so I ran from the Underground station. I feel better now, and I will tell you the facts as clearly as I can.

'Yesterday morning I was sitting in my office in the bank, when a card was brought in to me. I was surprised when I saw the name. It was one of the most famous names in England. I saw him immediately.

'"Mr Holder," he said, "I have been told that you lend money."

'"The company does lend money if we believe that the money will be repaid," I answered.

'"I need fifty thousand pounds immediately," he said, "I

could, of course, borrow such a small sum from my friends, but I prefer to make it a matter of business."

'"Can I ask you how long you want this sum for?"

'"Next Monday I shall receive a large amount of money. I shall certainly repay you then. But it is very important to me that the money is paid now."

'"I would be happy to lend you the money myself," I said, "but this amount is too large. If it comes from the company, I must ask you to leave something with us of the same value."

'"I would prefer that," he said, lifting up his square black leather case. "I am sure you have heard of the crown of diamonds."

'"It is one of the most valuable pieces of public property in this country," I said.

'"Exactly." He opened the case, and there, lying on soft pink cloth, was the beautiful piece of jewellery. "There are thirty-nine very large diamonds," he said, "and even the price of the gold is enormous. I will leave this crown with you." I took the case into my hands and looked doubtfully at the man. "You don't think it is right for me to leave it?" he asked. "I am certain that I will be able to take it back in four days. But please keep this matter secret, and take great care of the crown. I shall come for it on Monday morning."

'He was anxious to leave, so I arranged for the payment to him of fifty thousand pounds in notes. When I was alone again, I began to feel sorry that I had agreed to keep the valuable crown. It belonged to the nation, so there would be a terrible problem if anything happened to it. However, it was too late to change things now, so I locked it up in a special box in my room, and went back to my work.

'When evening came, I decided to take the crown home with me. Bankers' offices have been broken into before now. So I called a carriage and drove to my house in Streatham, carrying the crown with me. I did not breathe easily until I had taken it upstairs and locked it safely away in a cupboard in my dressing-room.

'I have two male servants, Mr Holmes, but they sleep out of the house, so we need not worry about them. I also have three excellent female servants who have been with me for a number of years.

'There is another servant, Lucy Parr, who has only been with me for a few months. However, she seems to be of good character, and she has always done her work well. She is a very pretty girl, and a number of young men have called on her. That is not a great problem, and we believe that she is a very good girl in every way.

'My family is small. My wife died some years ago, and I have only one son, called Arthur. He has caused me quite a lot of trouble. I blame myself completely. When my wife died, he was all that I loved. I gave him everything he wanted, and perhaps this was not good for him.

'I wanted Arthur to come and work with me in the bank, but he did not like business. When he was young, he became a member of a club and met a number of rich men with expensive habits. He began to lose money at cards and at the horse races, and he came to me again and again for more money. He tried many times to leave these new friends, but each time one man, Sir★ George Burnwell, pulled him back again.

'Sir George came frequently to the house at Streatham. I am not surprised that Arthur liked him, because he has been everywhere and done everything. He is a good talker, and very handsome, but I have never really liked him. My little Mary thinks the same way.

'Mary is my niece, but she is like my daughter. She came to live with us when my brother died five years ago. She is sweet,

★Sir: the title of a man from an important family.

41

loving and beautiful, and she takes care of the house. I do not know what I would do without her.

'She has only acted against my wishes in one thing. Twice my boy has asked her to marry him, because he loves her very much, and each time she has refused him. I thought that marriage to her might change his life, but now it is too late!

'Now, Mr Holmes, you know the people who live under my roof. I shall continue with my sad story.

'When we were having coffee after dinner that night, I told Arthur and Mary about the valuable crown that was now in the house. I did not tell them who had given it to me. Lucy Parr had brought in the coffee, and had left the room, but I cannot be sure that the door was closed. Mary and Arthur were very interested, and wanted to see the famous crown, but I did not show it to them.

' " Where have you put it? " Arthur asked.

' " In my dressing-room cupboard."

' " I hope nobody breaks into the house during the night," he said.

' " The cupboard is locked," I answered.

' " Oh, other keys will fit that cupboard. When I was a child I opened it with the key of the sitting-room cupboard."

'That night Arthur followed me to my room.

' " Dad," he said, with his eyes looking down, " can you let me have two hundred pounds? "

' " No, I cannot," I answered. " I have been too generous with you already."

' " You have been very kind," said Arthur, " but I must have the money, or I will not be able to enter the club again."

' " That would be a very good thing."

' " Yes, but you would not want me to leave it in shame," he said. " I could not live with that. I must get the money. If you will not give it to me, I must try something else."

'I was very angry, because this was the third demand in one month. "You will not have a penny from me," I shouted, and he turned and left the room.

'When he was gone I opened my cupboard, checked the crown, and locked it again. Then I went round the house, checking the locks on the doors and windows. I usually let Mary do this. As I came downstairs, I saw Mary at the side window of the hall. She closed and locked it when I came near.

'"Tell me, uncle," she said, looking a little anxious, "did you give Lucy permission to go out tonight?"

'"Certainly not."

'"She has just come in by the back door. She has probably only been to the side gate to see someone, but I think that it is not safe. We should stop it."

'"You or I must speak to her in the morning. Are you sure that everything is locked?"

'"Yes."

'"Then, good night." I kissed her, and went to my bedroom. Mr Holmes, I am not a very heavy sleeper, and I was worried about the crown. At about two in the morning, I was woken by a sound in the house.

'I had the idea that a window had gently closed somewhere. I listened and then suddenly heard, to my horror, the sound of soft footsteps in the next room. I got out of bed, very frightened, and looked round the door.

'"Arthur," I screamed, "you thief! What are you doing with that crown?"

'My son was standing beside the gaslight, holding the crown in his hands. He appeared to be bending it with all his strength. When I shouted, he dropped it and went as pale as death. I picked it up and examined it. One of the gold points, with three of the diamonds in it, had gone.

'"You horrible boy!" I shouted angrily. "You have destroyed

it! You have brought shame on me for ever! Where are the jewels you have stolen?"

' "Stolen!" he cried.

' " Yes, you thief!" I shouted, shaking him by the shoulder.

' " They are all there. They must all be there," he said.

' " Three have gone. And you know where they are. I saw you trying to pull off another piece."

' " You have insulted me enough," he said. " I will not listen. I will leave your house in the morning, and make my own way in the world."

' " You will leave in the hands of the police!" I cried, half mad with sadness and anger.

' " They will learn nothing from me," he said, and I have never seen him so angry. " If you decide to call the police, let them find what they can."

' By this time the whole house was awake, and Mary rushed into the room. At the sight of the crown and Arthur's face, she understood the whole story and fell to the floor. I sent for the police, and they arrived quickly. Arthur asked if I intended to let them take him away. I answered that it had become a public matter, since the crown belonged to the country.

' " It would," he said, " be to your advantage and mine if I could leave the house for five minutes first."

' " Then you could run away or perhaps hide what you have stolen," I said. " You have to face facts. You have been caught in the act, and nothing could make things worse for you. But tell me where the diamonds are. Then I shall forgive and forget everything."

' " I have not asked for your forgiveness," he answered, turning away from me. I called the police into the room and let them take him. A search was made, of Arthur, his room, and the house, but the stones were not found.

' This morning Arthur was taken to the police station, and I have hurried here to ask for your help. You can ask for as much money as you like. I have already offered a reward of a thousand pounds. My God, what shall I do? I have lost my good name, my diamonds and my son in one night. Oh, what shall I do!'

Sherlock Holmes sat silently for some minutes, staring into the fire.

'Do you have many guests in your house?' he asked.

'None, except for my business partner and his family, and sometimes Arthur's friends. Sir George Burnwell has been several times recently. No one else, I think.'

'Do you go out much?'

'Arthur does. Mary and I stay at home.'

'That is unusual for a young girl.'

'She is quiet. And she is not very young. She is twenty-four.'

'This business was a shock to her too.'

'A terrible shock!'

'And you both believe that your son is guilty?'

'I saw him with my own eyes with the crown in his hands.'

'That does not really prove anything. Was the rest of the crown damaged?'

'Yes, it was bent out of shape.'

'Do you not think that perhaps he was trying to straighten it again?'

'Mr Holmes, thank you! You are doing what you can for him and for me. But what was he doing there? If he had a good reason, why did he not say so?'

'Exactly. And if he was guilty, why didn't he invent a lie? Why did he keep silent? There are several puzzling points about this case. What did the police think about the noise that woke you from your sleep?'

'They thought it might be the sound of Arthur's bedroom door.'

'That is not likely. He would not make a noise if he was a

45

thief. What did they say about the disappearance of the diamonds?'

'They are still checking under the floors and in the furniture.'

'Have they looked outside?'

'Yes, they have examined the whole garden.'

'This matter, my dear sir,' said Holmes, 'is much more complicated than you or the police believe.

'You think that your son came from his bedroom to your dressing-room, opened your cupboard, took out your crown, broke off a small piece of it, went off to another place, hid three of the thirty-nine diamonds, and then returned to the dressing-room with the other thirty-six.'

'But what else is possible?' said the banker. 'If he is innocent, why doesn't he explain?'

'It is our job to solve that,' replied Holmes. 'So now, Mr Holder, we will go to Streatham together and spend an hour looking a little more closely at the details.'

My friend asked me to join them on the journey, which I very much wanted to do. It seemed to me that the son, Arthur, must be guilty, but Sherlock Holmes's judgement is almost always excellent.

Holmes spoke very little on the way to Streatham. He sat with his chin on his chest and his hat over his eyes, in deep thought. Mr Holder appeared happy with the fresh hope that Holmes had given him. He even talked to me about his business.

My friend only changed when we came in sight of Fairbank, the home of the great banker. He sat up and studied the house with great interest.

Fairbank was quite a large square house of white stone. A wide carriageway led down through the snow-covered garden to a large iron gate. On the right-hand side of this, there was a narrow path which led to the kitchen door. On the left a little road went to the back of the house, where the horses were kept. This was a

He sat up and studied the house with great interest.

public road, although it was not used much.

Holmes walked slowly all round the house, across the front, down the narrow path, across the garden and into the little road. Mr Holder and I went into the dining-room, and waited by the fire until he returned.

We were sitting there in silence when the door opened and a young lady came in. She was a little above middle-height, with light hair and blue eyes, though these were red with crying. Her face was very pale; even her lips were bloodless.

As she came into the room, she seemed even more unhappy than the banker had been that morning. She went straight to her uncle.

'You have given orders that Arthur should go free, haven't you?' she asked.

'No, no, my girl. The police must be satisfied that he is not guilty.'

'But I am sure he has done nothing.'

'Why is he silent, if he is innocent?'

'Who knows? Perhaps he was angry that you thought he did it.'

'How could I not think that, when he had the crown in his hand?'

'Oh, but he had only picked it up to look at it. Oh, believe me when I say that he is innocent. It is so terrible to think of our dear Arthur in prison!'

'I cannot free him until the diamonds are found, Mary! I have brought a gentleman from London to help me.'

'This gentleman?' she asked, looking at me.

'No. His friend. He wishes us to leave him alone. He is in the road at the side of the house now.'

'In the road? What can he hope to find there? Ah, this, I suppose, is him,' she said, as Holmes came into the room. 'I hope, sir, that you will prove my cousin Arthur's innocence.'

'I share your opinion, and agree that we must prove it,' Holmes said. 'I believe you are Miss Mary Holder. Can I ask you a question or two?'

'Please do, sir, if it will help to solve the puzzle.'

'You heard nothing yourself last night?'

'Nothing, until my uncle began to speak loudly.'

'You shut all the windows and doors the night before. Did you lock all the windows?'

'Yes.'

'Were they all locked this morning?'

'Yes.'

'You have a servant who has a male friend? I think you said to your uncle that she had been out to see him?'

'Yes, Lucy Parr. It is possible that she heard my uncle speak about the crown.'

'You are suggesting that she went out to tell her friend, and that the two of them planned to steal it.'

'But,' cried the banker, 'I have told you that I saw Arthur with the crown in his hands!'

'Wait, Mr Holder. We must come back to that. Miss Holder, did you see this girl return by the kitchen door?'

'Yes, I went to check the door, and I met her coming in. I saw the man, too, in the darkness.'

'Do you know him?'

'Oh yes, he is the man who brings our vegetables. His name is Francis Prosper.'

'He stood,' said Holmes, 'to the left of the door?'

'Yes, he did.'

'And he is a man with a wooden leg?'

Something like fear came into the young lady's eyes. 'How do you know that?' she asked. She smiled, but there was no answering smile in Holmes's thin face.

'I think I would like to go upstairs now,' he said. 'I shall probably want to look at the outside of the house again. Perhaps I shall look at the lower windows before I go up.'

He walked quickly round from one to the other, pausing only at the large one which looked from the hall to the little road at the side of the house. He opened this and examined it very carefully. 'Now we shall go upstairs,' he said at last.

The banker's dressing-room was quite small and contained only a dressing-table, a long mirror and a grey carpet. There was also a cupboard in the wall. Holmes went to this first and looked hard at the lock.

'Which key was used to open it?' he asked.

'The one which my son spoke about – from the cupboard in the sitting-room.'

'Do you have it here?'

'That is it on the dressing-table.'

Sherlock Holmes picked it up and opened the cupboard.

'It is a quiet lock,' he said. 'I am not surprised that it did not wake you. This case, I suppose, contains the crown. We must have a look at it.'

He opened the case and took out the piece of jewellery. It was a beautiful piece of work and the thirty-six stones were the finest I have ever seen. At one side of the crown there was a bent and broken edge. A point, with three diamonds, had been pulled off.

'Now, Mr Holder,' said Holmes, 'here is the opposite point to the one which has been lost. Can I ask you to break it off?'

The banker took a step back. 'I would not dream of trying,' he said.

'Then I will.' Holmes suddenly tried with all his strength to break the point off, but with no result. 'I can feel it move a little,' he said, 'and I have very strong fingers. An ordinary man could not do it.

'Now, what do you think would happen if I did break it, Mr Holder? There would be a noise like a gunshot. Are you telling

50

me this happened a few feet from your bed, and that you heard nothing?'

'I don't know what to think.'

'Did your son have shoes on when you saw him?'

'He had nothing on except his trousers and shirt.'

'Thank you. Well, I think we have had a lot of luck. It will be our fault if we do not succeed in solving this case. With your permission, Mr Holder, I shall go outside again.'

He went alone, explaining that extra footprints might make his work more difficult. For an hour or more he was at work.

'I think I have now seen everything, Mr Holder,' he said, when he came back. 'I shall now return to my rooms.'

'But the diamonds, Mr Holmes. Where are they?'

'I do not know.'

'I shall never see them again,' the banker cried. 'And my son? Can you give me any hope?'

'My opinion has not changed.'

'Then what happened in this house last night?'

'If you can visit my Baker Street rooms tomorrow morning between nine and ten, I shall try to make it clearer. Can I do anything that is necessary to get the diamonds back? There must be no limit to the money I can spend.'

'I would give all my money to have them back,' the banker replied.

'Very good. Goodbye – though it is possible that I may come here again before evening.'

Part 2   The Detective's Solution

Several times during our journey home, I tried to make my friend tell me his thoughts about the case. But he always changed the subject, and at last I stopped asking.

It was before three when we found ourselves in our rooms again. Holmes hurried to his bedroom, but soon returned. He was dressed like a man who might be looking for work, in an old coat and older boots.

'I think that this will be all right,' he said, looking in the mirror above the fireplace. 'I am sorry that you cannot come with me, but I do not think it would be wise. I hope to be back in a few hours.' He cut some meat from the piece on the table, made himself a sandwich, put this into his pocket and left the room.

I had just finished my tea when he returned. He was looking very satisfied and holding an old boot in his hand. He threw this down into a corner and took a cup of tea.

'I am going out again,' he said.

'Where to?'

'Oh, the other side of London. Don't wait up for me.'

'How are you doing?'

'Quite well. I have been out to Streatham, but I did not visit the house. It is an interesting little problem and I am very glad that it came to me. However, I must not sit here talking. I must change my clothes and return to my normal appearance.'

His eyes were shining, and there was even a little colour in his normally pale face. He hurried upstairs, and a few minutes later I heard the hall door close.

I waited until midnight, but then I went to bed. I do not know when he came in, but he was there at breakfast with a cup of coffee in one hand and the newspaper in the other.

'Please excuse me, Watson,' he said. 'I started without you, because Mr Holder is coming quite early this morning.'

'Yes. It is after nine now,' I answered, 'and there is the sound of the bell.'

When the banker came in, I was shocked by the change in him. His face looked quite thin and his hair seemed to be whiter than before. He walked in a slow, tired way that was even more painful than the violence of his entry the morning before. He fell heavily into the chair which I pushed forward for him.

'Only two days ago I was a very happy man,' he said. 'Now the last years of my life will be lonely and unhappy. One bad thing follows another – my niece Mary has left me.'

'Left you?'

'Yes. Her bed this morning had not been slept in. Her room was empty, and there was a note for me on the hall table. I said last night that I was sorry she didn't marry my boy. Perhaps I was wrong to say that. This is her note:

My dear uncle,

I feel that my actions are the cause of your trouble. I cannot ever be happy again under your roof, so I must leave you. Do not worry about my future, because that is arranged, and do not search for me. In life or in death, I am your loving

Mary

'What does she mean by that note, Mr Holmes? Do you think she might kill herself?'

'No, no, nothing like that. It is perhaps the best possible solution. You are, Mr Holder, coming to the end of your troubles.'

'Ha! You have heard something, Mr Holmes! You have learned something! Where are the diamonds?'

'A thousand pounds each would not be too much to pay for them?'

'I would pay ten.'

'That would be unnecessary. Three thousand will be enough. And there is a little reward, I think. Have you your cheque-book? Here is a pen.'

With a surprised look on his face, the banker wrote a cheque for four thousand pounds. Holmes walked to his desk, took out a little piece of gold with three diamonds in it, and threw it down on the table.

With a cry of happiness, the banker picked up the broken piece from the crown of diamonds.

'You have it?' he whispered.'I am saved! I am saved!'

'There is one other thing that you owe, Mr Holder,' said Sherlock Holmes.

'Owe?' The banker picked up the pen. 'Name the amount, and I will pay it.'

'No, it is not money that you owe. Your son is a very fine boy. You should be proud of him, and you must now apologize to him.'

'So Arthur did not take them?'

'I told you yesterday, and I repeat today, that he did not.'

'You are sure of it! Then let us hurry to him. We shall tell him that the truth has been found.'

'He knows it already. I had an interview with him. He did not want to tell me the story, so I told it to him. He had to agree that I was right. He added the few details that were not clear to me. Your news of this morning, however, may open his lips.'

'Then please tell me what this mystery is about!'

'I will tell you, but first I must tell you something else. Sir George Burnwell and your niece, Mary, have run away together.'

'My Mary? Impossible!'

'It is, unfortunately, certain. You and your son did not know the true character of this man. He is one of the most dangerous men in England. He has lost large amounts of money on cards and horses. He is a man without a heart.

'When he told your niece that he loved her, she believed him. She did not know that he had said the same thing to a hundred women before her. She saw him nearly every evening.'

'I cannot and I will not believe it!' cried the banker, with a white face.

'*When he told your niece that he loved her, she believed him.*'

'I will tell you, then, what happened in your house that night. When your niece thought you had gone to your room, she went downstairs. She talked to her lover through the window which looks into the little road by the side of the house. He had stood there for a very long time, so his footprints had pressed right through the snow.

'She told him about the crown, and he wanted it very much. I have no doubt that she loved you, but he had a strong power over her. She saw you coming downstairs again, so she closed the window quickly and told you about the servant and her wooden-legged lover. That was all perfectly true.

'Your boy, Arthur, went to bed after his interview with you, but he slept badly because he was worried about money. In the middle of the night he heard a soft step pass his door. He got up, looked out, and was surprised to see his cousin walking very quietly along the passage.

'He quickly put on some clothes and waited there in the dark to watch. Very soon she came out of the room and, in the light of the passage lamp, your son saw that she was carrying the crown in her hands. She walked down the stairs and he waited behind the curtain near your door. From there he could see everything that happened in the hall below.

'He saw her quietly open the window, give the crown to someone standing outside, and then close it and hurry back to her room.

'He realized immediately how bad this would be for you. He rushed down the stairs, without his shoes, opened the window, jumped out into the snow, and ran down the road. Sir George Burnwell tried to get away, but Arthur caught him. There was a fight between them. Your son pulled at one side of the crown and Sir George at the other.

'In the fight, your son hit Sir George and cut him over the eye. Then something suddenly broke, and Arthur found the crown in his hands. He rushed back, closed the window and went up to your dressing-room. When you came in, he had just noticed that the crown had been bent in the fight. He was trying to straighten it.'

'Is it possible?' whispered the banker.

'You then insulted him when he felt he deserved your warmest thanks. He could not tell you the truth without getting Mary into trouble. She had done nothing to deserve it, but he kept her secret.'

'She was shocked when she saw the crown,' cried Mr Holder. 'Oh, my God! I have been a blind fool! And he asked me to let him out for five minutes! The dear boy wanted to look for the missing piece at the scene of the fight.'

'When I arrived at the house,' continued Holmes, 'I went very carefully round it and looked at the prints in the snow. I knew that no snow had fallen since the evening before.

'I went along the narrow path, but too many people had walked on it. Just beyond it, however, at the far side of the kitchen door, a woman had stood and talked with a man. The round print on one side showed that he had a wooden leg.

'She had to leave him quickly, because she had run back to the door, leaving deep toe prints and light heel prints. Wooden-leg had waited a little, and then had gone away. I thought at the time that this might be the servant girl and her lover. I learned from you that it was.

'I then looked at the little road at the side of the house, and found a long and interesting story written in the snow. There was a double line of prints of a man wearing boots, and a second double line made by a man with no shoes on his feet. I was sure, from our conversation in the morning, that this second man was your son.

'The first had walked both ways, but the other man had run quickly. In some places his prints went over the prints of the boots, so I could see that he had come after the other one. The prints led to the hall window.

'Then I walked to the other end, down in the road. I saw where Boots had turned round. It seemed that there had been a fight. Finally, I found some blood, and I knew that I was right.

'Boots had then run down the road, and more blood showed that he had been hurt. At the other end of the road, the snow had been cleared, so I could not follow him.

'When I entered the house, I examined the hall window. I could see at once that someone had gone out through it. I could also see the print of a wet foot coming in.

'I was then beginning to understand what had happened. A man had waited outside the window and someone had brought him the crown. Your son had seen this and had followed the thief. They had fought, and pulled at the crown. The strength of both of them had bent it.

'Your son had returned to the house with the crown, but had left a piece with the other man. All this was clear. The questions now were: Who was the other man? And who had brought him the crown?

'When you take away the impossible, you are left with the truth, although the truth often seems very unlikely. I knew that you had not brought the crown down, so it was your niece or Lucy Parr. But why would your son take the blame for Lucy's actions?

'There was no possible reason. But his love for his cousin was an excellent reason for keeping her secret. I remembered that you had seen her at that window. I also remembered that she was shocked when she saw the crown in your son's hands. Then I was sure I was right.

'And who could the other person be? A lover, of course. Who else could make her forget her love for you? I knew that you did not go out much, but one of your visitors was Sir George

Burnwell. I had heard of his behaviour with women. It seemed quite likely that he had the diamonds.

'Well, I went to his house yesterday, dressed as a poor man. I spoke to one of his servants and I learned that Sir George had been out all the night before. Finally, I bought a pair of his old shoes. I took them to Streatham, and they were exactly the same size as the footprints.'

'I saw someone in the little road by the house yesterday evening,' said Mr Holder.

'Yes, that was me. I knew who the criminal was, and I went to see him. At first, of course, he denied everything. But when I told him all the details, he picked up a heavy stick and came towards me.

'I pointed a revolver at his head before he could hit me. Then he decided to be sensible. I told him that I would give him a thousand pounds for each of the diamonds. I also promised him that he would hear nothing more about the matter.

'"Oh no!" he said. "I have sold all three for six hundred pounds!" He gave me the address of the man he had sold them to. After some discussion, I managed to get the stones for a thousand pounds each.

'Then I visited your son Arthur and told him the good news. I went to bed at two o'clock in the morning, after a really hard day's work.'

'A day which has saved England from great public shame!' said the banker. He got up from his chair. 'Sir, I cannot find the words to thank you. Your skill is even greater than people say. And now I must go and apologize to my dear boy. Your news about poor Mary hurts me greatly. Not even your skill can tell me where she is now.'

'I think we can be sure,' replied Holmes, 'that she is in the same place as Sir George Burnwell. We can also be sure that she will soon be punished enough.'

ACTIVITIES

The Speckled Band

Before you read

1 In this story a woman dies saying the words, 'It was the band! The speckled band!' Sherlock Holmes tries to guess what killed her. What do you think? Find the word *speckled* in your dictionary. Then choose one of these four meanings of the word *band*. Which ones can be speckled?

   a a group of people with the same interests

   b a group of musicians

   c a thick coloured line

   d something long and narrow that forms a circle

2 Each of these words has a meaning which connects it with one or more of the words in *italics*. Which words? Use your dictionary to help you. The words in *italics* are all in the story.

   fire ....   sound ....   clothes .....

   crime ....   building ....

   candle   case   hiss   poker   revolver   shutters   veil   ventilate whistle

3 Write the best word in each space. Use your dictionary to help you.

   carriage   horror   however   inn   lead   owe   passage   rope snake   stepfather   will

   a Cinderella arrived at the dance in a ..... . She walked along the ..... to the dance hall. She enjoyed the dance. At midnight, ..., she had to leave. When she arrived home, she saw, to her ..... , that she had lost a shoe.

   b The ..... had a lot of regular customers. One of them was my ..... . He ..... a lot of money for drinks, but he never paid his bill. When he died, we read his ..... . In it, he asked us to pay his bar bill.

61

c Charlie had two pets. He kept a ….. in the sitting-room, but he really loved his dog. He took it for walks on a ….. that was made from an old ….. .

After you read

4 In this story, the background to the murder is quite important. Which information in sentences 1–6 leads to the result in sentences a–f?

1 Dr Roylott was a doctor of medicine.

2 Dr Roylott was interested in Indian animals.

3 Dr Roylott killed a man in India.

4 Dr Roylott spent a number of years in prison.

5 Mrs Stoner was killed in a railway accident.

6 The family did not have enough money to repair the whole house.

a Dr Roylott was able to give up working.

b Dr Roylott returned to England, a very sad and angry man.

c Dr Roylott knew how to hold snakes.

d Dr Roylott had murdered once, and might be able to do so again.

e The bedrooms in the house were next door to each other.

f Dr Roylott knew about poisons and how they work.

The Five Orange Pips

Before you read

5 Try to find some information about the history of the United States. This information is important to the story.

a What happened between 1861 and 1865?

b The name 'Jackson' appears in the story. He was an important man at that time. Who was he?

6 Answer the questions. Find the words in *italics* in your dictionary.

  a Where might you find a:

    – *footprint*?

    – *lawyer*?

    – *pip*?

  b What do you do with a:

    – *puzzle*?

    – *violin*?

  c What is the opposite of:

    – tell the *truth*?

After you read

7 Work with two other students. The *Lone Star* is sailing up the River Thames towards London. Continue this conversation between the ship's three officers:

Captain Calhoun: We must send the pips to John Openshaw.

1st Officer: We're taking a chance if we do that. We've already killed twice, and we got away. We might not be so lucky this time.

2nd Officer: I say we should let him live. He may not have the papers. And if he does have them, he won't understand them.

The Crown of Diamonds

Part 1

Before you read

8 Find these words in your dictionary. Which is a word for an emotion? What makes you feel this way?

crown   shame

9 What might happen to a crown of diamonds? What might Sherlock Holmes's job be in this case?

10 Look at this page from Sherlock Holmes's notebook:

The crown – who stole it?

Arthur   So why bring it back?

Mary   Why? Doesn't need money.

Lucy   Thinking of marriage? May need money.

Why is Arthur silent? Who has the missing piece?

Discuss who stole the crown, and why.

Part 2

Before you read

11 When he arrives at Mr Holder's house, Sherlock Holmes does these things. Why, do you think?

a He spends a long time walking around the garden.

b He opens a large window which looks from the hall to the road by the side of the house and examines it carefully.

c He tries to break off another piece of the crown.

After you read

12 Work with another student. Have this conversation.

Student A: You are Sherlock Holmes. You know now what happened, but you want Arthur to tell you everything.

Student B: You are Arthur. You do not want to say anything until you understand that Holmes knows most of the story. Then you are ready to give extra details.

Writing

13 (*The Speckled Band*) You are a police officer and you have to write a report on the death of Julia Stoner. This should include details of Dr Roylott's character and behaviour, and a description of the family and of the house, with special attention to her room. You can give your own ideas about how she died. (You know nothing about the snake!)

14 (*The Speckled Band*) Imagine that Dr Roylott does not die at the end of the story. Instead, he is taken to court for murder. There is no doubt that he is guilty. However, he may not be killed for the murder if his lawyer can show that he is mad. Write the lawyer's speech.

15 (*The Five Orange Pips*) Some time after the *Lone Star* has sunk, another box with the letters K.K.K. on it is found in the sea. A notebook inside contains Captain Calhoun's story of the death of John Openshaw. Write his story.

16 (*The Five Orange Pips*) After the *Lone Star* sails, Holmes wants to tell the Savannah police that the three officers are wanted in England for murder. Imagine that he goes to see Lestrade, of the London police. Holmes has helped Lestrade in the past, but there are not very many facts to prove that the deaths were murder. Holmes has to make Lestrade believe that the Savannah police should send the men back to England. Write their conversation.

17 (*The Crown of Diamonds*) Write the conversation that Mary has with Sir George Burnwell through the open window on the night when the diamonds disappear.

18 (*The Crown of Diamonds*) On the morning after the crown is returned, Mr Holder takes it to his office. He must take it to a jeweller for repairs, and the bank will have to pay. So first he must write a report for his partner – but he wants to protect his family. Write his report.

Answers for the Activities in this book are available from your local office or alternatively write to: Penguin Readers Marketing Department, Pearson Education, Edinburgh Gate, Harlow, Essex CM20 2JE.